BEARS IN THE WILD

AN AUDUBON READER

BEARS IN THE WILD

ADA AND FRANK GRAHAM
ILLUSTRATED BY D. D. TYLER

DELACORTE PRESS / NEW YORK

Published by
Delacorte Press
1 Dag Hammarskjold Plaza
New York, N.Y. 10017

Manufactured in the United States of America

First printing

Library of Congress Cataloging in Publication Data

Graham, Ada.
Bears in the wild.
(An Audubon reader; 6)
Bibliography: p.
Includes index.
SUMMARY: Discusses bears around the world,
particularly in the United States, and the necessity
of providing them with sufficient space before
they disappear altogether.
1. Bears—Juvenile literature. [1. Bears]
I. Graham, Frank, 1925– joint author.
II. Tyler, D. D. III. Title. IV. Series:
Audubon reader; 6.
QL737.C27G73   599.74′446   80–68732
ISBN 0–440–00532–9
ISBN 0–440–00538–8 (lib. bdg.)

To the memory of Marie Rodell,
conservationist and helpful friend
to so many of us who write about the natural world,
this book is dedicated.

CONTENTS

INTRODUCTION
A WORD ABOUT BEARS

People have a hard time making up their minds about bears. Some are frightened to death of them. Others believe they are cute and cuddly, and would probably walk right up to a big bear in the forest and hand it a bag of potato chips. But, whether people look on them with fear or friendliness, they are always interested in bears.

Bears belong to a family of animals that scientists call the *Ursidae*. This name comes from *ursus*, which is the Latin word for bear. They are distant relatives of the dog family. Until very recently bears were widespread across all the northern continents of the world—Europe, Asia, and North America. Only one species, or kind, the spectacled bear, lives in South America. Bears do not live in Africa or Australia. The animal that is sometimes mistakenly called a koala bear is really a relative of the opossum.

The world's seven species of bears look very much alike except for the color of their fur. They are large, powerfully built animals with a fairly long muzzle and a very short tail. They have sturdy legs and five toes on each broad foot.

Bears have rather small heads in comparison to their heavy bodies. The small, rounded ears are set well back on the head, giving these animals, in the words of one naturalist, "an almost comical look."

Perhaps this comical look is one of the reasons why people find bears so appealing. A stronger reason, however, is that bears often move in such a way that they remind us of human beings.

"Doesn't that bear walk just like our friend so-and-so!" someone will say on a visit to the zoo, and all the other people laugh because they can see the resemblance.

Bears walk in a rolling, flat-footed way, as some people do. They are able to fall back on their haunches and sit upright, as if they are seated on a chair. In that position they pick up and handle food or other objects with almost the same dexterity as a human. They stretch out on their backs as lazily as a fat man taking a sunbath. Finally, they sometimes stand erect on their hind legs and walk easily and almost gracefully. Human beings

People now realize that bears, like this polar bear and her cubs, are attractive and intelligent animals.

have always felt a close kinship to bears, penguins, and other animals that are able to walk upright.

It is easy to think of bears as people. The three bears that Goldilocks visited seem real to many children. Winnie-the-Pooh is as bumbling but lovable as many people we know.

One of the most popular toys ever made is the teddy bear. It was named for President Theodore (Teddy) Roosevelt. Roosevelt went on a hunting trip in 1902. He discovered a black bear cub he liked so much that he captured it and took it back to his camp. A newspaper cartoonist drew a picture of the bear and called it Teddy, after the President. A toy manufacturer asked Roosevelt's permission to use the picture as a model for a stuffed toy bear. Since then, millions of children have enjoyed the company of a teddy bear.

Almost fifty years later a great forest fire blazed out of control in New Mexico. Many animals died, but rangers rescued a black bear cub from the flames. They called him Smokey and used his picture on posters and in advertisements to warn people to be careful about starting fires. The message of Smokey the Bear, who always wore a forest ranger's hat in those pictures, helped to prevent fires. He was finally sent to live in the Washington Zoo, where he became a great favorite with visitors.

Bears have given people a great deal of pleasure. But

only in recent times have we begun to understand these attractive and intelligent animals. This book tries to increase that understanding by describing, in some detail, the lives of the two species that are most common in North America—the grizzly and the black bear.

Bears are in serious danger of disappearing from many parts of the world, and only by putting to use our new knowledge can we save the ones that are left.

1
GRIZZLY

One day in 1860 Phineas T. Barnum, who created the Barnum & Bailey Circus, received a strange visitor in his New York office.

"He was dressed in his hunter's suit of buckskin, trimmed with the skins and bordered with the hanging tails of small Rocky Mountain animals," Barnum wrote. "His cap consisted of the skin of a wolf's head and shoulders, from which hung several tails. Under these appeared his stiff, bushy, gray hair and his long, white, grizzly beard. In fact, Old Adams was quite as much of a show as his beasts."

The man who visited Barnum that day was the famous western hunter and trapper, Grizzly Adams. He had just arrived in New York from California. With him he had brought his own collection of wild animals. These animals, which he kept in cages, included more than twenty fierce grizzly bears, several wolves, mountain lions, buffaloes, and a large sea lion.

There was no easy way to cross the American continent in those days. Grizzly Adams had packed his animals aboard a ship in San Francisco and sailed around the tip of South America to New York. Even after the long sea voyage, the animals looked much healthier to Barnum than Adams did.

"During our conversation, Grizzly Adams took off his cap and showed me the top of his head," Barnum wrote. "His skull was broken in. It had been struck a number of times by the fearful paws of his grizzly students. The last blow, from the bear called General Fremont, had laid open his brain so that its workings were plainly visible."

Barnum was a master showman. He agreed to put on a performance that would star Grizzly Adams and his animals. But he wondered how this badly injured man could take part in such a show.

"Mr. Barnum, I am not the man I was five years ago," Adams told him. "Then I felt able to stand the hug of any

---

These three species of bears—from top to bottom, the grizzly, polar, and black bear—have different shaped heads and snouts.

3

grizzly bear. I was always glad to fight any sort of an animal."

Barnum knew that this man was only forty-eight years old. Yet he looked like an old man.

"I have been beaten to a jelly, torn almost limb from limb," Adams told him. "I have been nearly chewed up and spit out by these treacherous grizzly bears. But I am good for a few months yet. By that time I hope I shall earn enough money to make my wife comfortable."

Barnum put up an enormous tent in downtown New York. Thousands of people bought tickets to see Grizzly Adams and the wild animals he had captured in the West.

There was a colorful parade down Broadway on the morning that the show opened. A brass band, playing blood-stirring tunes, led the parade. Horses pulled the caged animals.

The crowds that lined the street saw an amazing sight. Riding on a platform was Grizzly Adams. He was dressed in the suit made of the skins and tails of animals. With him on the platform were three big grizzly bears. He sat on the back of the largest grizzly and held the other two bears on thick chains.

Grizzly Adams became a great favorite with New Yorkers. Newspaper articles described his adventures. The public learned that he had been born in Medway, Massachusetts, and as a young man he had worked as a shoemaker. But he had always liked to hunt in the woods of northern New England. When his business failed, he went to California, where he became a hunter and trapper.

Adams was afraid of nothing. Once a grizzly attacked him in the forest, splitting his head open with a blow of its powerful paw. But Adams wounded the bear with his gun and then killed it with his long hunting knife.

Grizzly Adams built traps for the large animals that lived in the mountains. He captured many bears and took them to San Francisco. There he tried to tame them to appear in wild animal shows. People flocked to see this fearless man enter the arena with his grizzly bears.

But a large wild animal can never really be tamed. There is always a spark of wildness that remains. Once in a while one of the bears would turn on Adams and batter him with a sharp-clawed paw. The bears broke his bones and tore his body. When he recovered from his wounds, however, he always returned to his animals.

The public was fascinated by Adams, but when they came to see him they also became fascinated by the huge animals he had tried to tame. Their speed and strength were amazing. People who lived in the cities had never dreamed that such wildness existed. There was something noble in the power and ferocity of these animals.

Grizzly Adams was not able to go on very long. Only a

6

few months after he brought his animals to New York, he died of the wounds they had inflicted on him. But in a way he lives on in our own time, for movies and television continue to tell the story of his adventurous life.

The grizzly bears he fought and tried to tame still interest us too. They have disappeared from the places where Grizzly Adams hunted them. Like most other members of the widespread family of bears, they find it harder and harder to exist in a world that is dominated by human beings.

Human beings have always felt a close kinship to bears and other animals that are able to walk upright.

2
BEARS, NATIVE AMERICANS, AND RANCHEROS

California can be called "the Grizzly Bear State." The bear's likeness appears on both the flag and the great seal of the state, and the legislature named it the state animal. More than two hundred settlements, streams, valleys, and other places in California are named for grizzlies. The sports teams at the University of California are called the Golden Bears. And those at the University of California at Los Angeles are called the Bruins, which is another name for bears.

But something has happened to the bears. No one has seen a wild grizzly in California for almost sixty years.

Grizzly bears played an important and colorful part in California's history, for they once existed there in great numbers. Why then were these interesting animals completely wiped out? As we try to answer that question, we will learn a lot about grizzly bears. We will also learn a lot about human beings.

Grizzlies, as we shall see, are just one of the many kinds of bears that are found all around the world. They are members of the same species of brown bears that at one time lived in much of Europe and Asia. Some of these bears crossed the old land bridge that once connected Asia with Alaska and spread over parts of this continent. After many centuries they grew to be much larger than their relatives in their old home on the other side of the world.

The grizzly bear differs from the black bear, which is so much more common in most of North America. It is larger and fiercer. Its claws are longer. Its dark-brown or reddish hairs are light-colored near their tips. This sharp difference in the coloring of its fur gives it a "grizzled" look and so accounts for its name.

The earliest humans who settled on the West Coast of North America quickly learned to live with these shaggy monsters. A native American warrior, with his primitive weapons, was no match for a healthy grizzly. If an especially ferocious, or "rogue," bear attacked and killed one of the tribe, the warriors knew they must defend themselves. In that case, they often formed a party and tracked down the killer bear.

But usually the Indian tribes left the grizzlies alone.

The light tips of this bear's fur give it a "grizzled" look.

They learned that even the largest grizzly would generally ignore them unless it was surprised or attacked.

The native Americans, however, did have a conflict of a different kind with the grizzlies. They both liked the same kinds of foods. Early in the summer the Indians in some California tribes ate nourishing wild plants such as clover, and in the fall they gathered acorns from oak trees to provide food during the cold months.

Grizzly bears spent much of their time searching for these foods too. Often they entered the meadows where the tastiest plants grew. They roamed the forest where acorns were plentiful. The Indians did not dare to challenge the bears, and sometimes these animals took the better part of the crop.

The figure of the bear played a large part in native American culture. In many parts of North America, the Indians ruled the land. They were strong enough and clever enough to conquer any wild beast. But in California, where grizzly bears were numerous, the Indians usually were forced to give way before their superior strength.

They believed that no creature on earth was as powerful or as wicked as a grizzly. Among the Wintun Indians, the most horrible curse one warrior could put on another was to say: "May the grizzly bear bite off your father's head!"

Two biologists, Tracy Storer and Lloyd Tevis, made a study of the Indians' attitude toward these animals for their book *California Grizzly*. They learned that while many tribes feared grizzlies, they also admired them.

The Indians lived among bears and were able to observe them closely. The bears impressed the tribes by how nearly they resembled human beings in the way they moved about and handled objects. In a way, the Indians looked on the bears as people, "but very bad people."

Some tribes buried their dead wrapped in the skins of grizzlies. Other tribes believed that a person who died would return to life as a grizzly. Bear doctors, or *shamans*, were powerful members of the tribe who dressed in bearskins and were believed to take on the power of these animals. They were said to use their magical power against the tribe's enemies.

The coming of the Spaniards to the Southwest did not change this picture very much. After the Europeans discovered America, California became a part of the Spanish colony of Mexico. A few Spanish explorers had seen California, but for nearly three hundred years after Columbus found the New World the Spaniards did little to settle this region.

Then, in 1776, just at the time that the United States was becoming a new nation, colonists entered California from Mexico. They arrived with their horses and their herds of cattle, adding these large animals to the California environment. They divided the land into ranches of great size.

By the year 1830 the *rancheros*, as the ranchers were called, owned flourishing herds of cattle and other domestic animals. The style of life did not change when Mexico won its independence from Spain. The Spanish flag was taken down and the Mexican flag flew over California.

Grizzly bears flourished right along with the *rancheros*, for the thousands of cattle that grazed the California land gave the bears an abundant new source of food. The bears found it was easy to kill these domestic animals. They also fed on any cattle that died on the range.

Under these conditions, the bears grew in number. They did not fear the Spaniards, any more than they had feared the Indians. They strolled across their ranches or into their settlements. The people fled in terror.

The Spanish-speaking people were not great hunters, as the English-speaking colonists were in the East. Only soldiers and a few important people were allowed to own guns in California. But the grizzlies did not seriously threaten the *rancheros* they met in the countryside. The *rancheros* rode everywhere on horseback and escaped almost any animal that attacked them.

But if the *rancheros* did not hunt with guns, they brought many grizzly bears to grief in another way. They were experts in the use of a long rope made of rawhide, or the skins of cattle, called a *reata*. It was knotted and thrown just like the American cowboy throws a lasso to catch horses and cattle.

The *rancheros* learned to capture grizzlies with a *reata*. It was a dangerous sport, practiced with the aid of their horses. In *California Grizzly*, Storer and Tevis quoted an early writer who watched the *rancheros* handle a *reata*:

"When one of these men wants to use his rope against a man or an animal, he holds it coiled in his hand. He goes at a gallop to within fifteen paces of his enemy, while making the cord turn above his head like a sling. At the proper moment, he throws it with so much skill that he never fails to catch his victim by the neck, body or legs. Then he drags him with great cruelty over the ground, at his horse's utmost speed."

The *rancheros* captured many bears. It took great courage to ride up to a grizzly and catch it with the *reata*. They had to watch the animal constantly. One slip and both horse and rider could be smashed to the ground by a blow from the bear's dreadful paw.

A *ranchero* named Ramon Carrillo used quick thinking

to save his life. One day, when he was trying to catch a bear, the huge animal fell into a deep pit. Man and horse, following closely, fell into the pit with the bear.

The bear, confused by the sudden fall, turned and tried to scramble up the wall of the pit. Carrillo, who knew that he had no chance of fighting the bear without a weapon, used his wits instead. He simply put both hands on the bear's rear end and pushed. Helped by this boost, the bear reached the top of the pit and ran away!

Many times, when the *rancheros* captured a bear, they forced it to take part in a cruel sport. They staged a deadly fight between the bear and a bull. Large crowds attended these fights, which were often held in a town square on Sunday after church.

The bulls on California ranches were savage animals similar to those used in Spanish bullfights. They had long, sharp horns that they thrust with deadly accuracy at a man or another animal. The bull and the bear were tied together by a strong rope so that they could not run away from each other.

The bull had to win quickly, or not at all. Its only chance was to rush at the bear and gore it in the body with a razor-sharp horn. But usually the bear survived the bull's charge. Then it would grasp the bull's face in its crushing jaws. As the crowd shrieked in excitement, the bear slowly exhausted its enemy and either killed it outright or injured it so badly that it bled to death.

The grizzly bear was still the king of California, both in the arena and in the countryside. By the 1840s there were more than ten thousand grizzlies in that region, probably more than there had ever been before.

No one would have believed that their doom was a matter of only a few years.

3

A DEADLY COLLISION

The tide of settlement overflowed the original thirteen United States and rolled rapidly westward. It did not take long for the new Americans to realize that the West offered bright opportunities for adventurous people.

Part of the knowledge about this region was provided by an expedition that President Thomas Jefferson sent out in 1804. The explorers Meriwether Lewis and William Clark led their party across the country to the shores of the Pacific Ocean. Lewis and Clark discovered many marvelous mountains and rivers, as well as plants and animals.

No animal impressed these explorers more than the grizzly bear. Meriwether Lewis met one of these mighty beasts on the banks of a river. He opened fire on the bear, putting ten bullets into its body. Five of the bullets passed through the bear's lungs. Yet the snarling, wounded animal swam off across the river and did not die for another twenty minutes.

Stories spread rapidly about this frightening but admirable animal. Some people believed that the stories were "tall tales," but the bear seemed to be a very real threat to the early settlers who disturbed it in its territory. If attacked, a grizzly seldom retreated. It rose on its hind legs, lashing out with the crushing power of its paws to meet the attack of even a heavily armed man.

Trapper and mountain man Jedediah Smith was fearless. Used to dealing with big wild animals, Smith thought he could conquer any bear. But one day a grizzly knocked his gun aside. A man who was with Smith described what happened.

"The bear had taken nearly all of his head in his great mouth close to his left eye on one side and close to his right ear on the other," the man wrote afterward. "He laid the skull bare to near the crown of his head. He left a white streak where his teeth passed, and one of Smith's ears was torn from his head to the outer rim."

Jedediah Smith recovered, but other hunters who attacked a grizzly did not live to brag about it.

The Far West was lightly settled until 1849. Besides

the Indian tribes, only a few *rancheros*, missionaries, soldiers, and trappers lived in California. But in that year gold was discovered in the Sacramento Valley. Thousands of people, expecting to find immense riches, rushed to California from the East. A head-on collision between the newcomers and the most powerful creature in that land, the grizzly bear, took place.

At first the bears were hunted chiefly as a source of fresh meat in places where supplies were scarce. Bear steaks began to appear on menus in the restaurants where gold miners ate. A special treat was bear paws, which the miners described as being sweet and tender.

In a boarding school that was opened for the children of settlers, the teacher used bear oil to dress her hair. According to the authors of *California Grizzly*, who retold this story, the children didn't mind this very much. But some of them objected when they learned that she was frying their pancakes in the same oil.

People who became farmers or ranchers followed the gold miners west. The struggle against grizzlies became more bitter. The bears, who never were seriously troubled by the Indians or the Spanish-speaking people, showed not the least fear of the latest arrivals.

The struggle was not yet completely one-sided. In the hands of the settlers the old-fashioned guns packed little

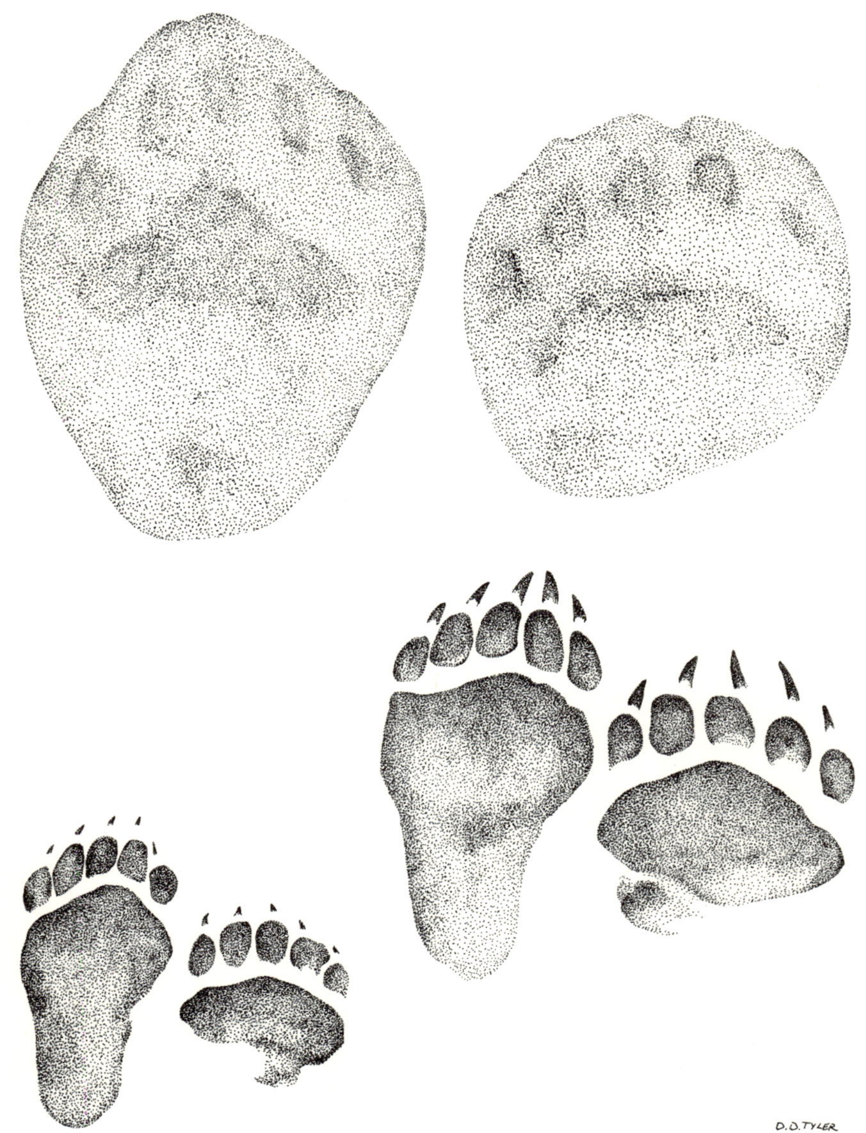

22

of the power of a modern rifle. Often the bullets failed to pierce the thick layer of fat that encased a bear's body. The slightly wounded bear would become enraged and was likely to kill or maim the hunter.

Grizzlies invaded many farms and ranches. They frightened the owners and killed the livestock. Just as westerners sometimes formed posses to capture cattle rustlers, the California settlers rode out together on horseback to track down grizzlies. They brought dogs on the hunt to help with the tracking.

A man who lived in the West during the 1840s described one of those bear hunts, and his tale has been quoted by Storer and Tevis in *California Grizzly*. The hunters, with their dogs and horses, entered the thick brush along a river. One of the riders was mounted on an inexperienced horse. Serious trouble began when the colt entered the thicket:

"The grizzly, disturbed in its lair, made straight for the horseman. The colt, being frightened, stood as if paralyzed until too late. It received a blow from the bear that knocked it down. The rider was seized before he

---

At the top are the tracks of a polar bear. The soles of its feet are covered with stiff hairs to keep it from slipping on the ice. The tracks on the lower right belong to a grizzly, the smaller ones on the lower left to a black bear.

could rise and the flesh was torn from the bone of his arm.

"At this critical moment, when it seemed that nothing could save the unfortunate man's life, there came out of the bushes another form like a flash of light. With one bound it landed on the back of the enraged grizzly. Then it seized the bear's hindquarters in its teeth.

"This new combatant was a dog. He forced the bear to defend itself from the attack in the rear. Who has not seen a dog try to catch its own tail? He who has can imagine the bear trying to get hold of 'Tinker,' its attacker.

"The dog hung to the grizzly's haunch like grim death, shaking it, growling with fury. As the bear rushed in circles, the dog looked like an overgrown bear's tail that the owner was frantically trying to lay hold of, if it could ever turn around fast enough to catch up with it.

"One of the hunters spurred his horse between the combatants and the fallen man, who, springing to his feet, made a successful retreat out of harm's way. A few well-directed bullets put an end to the bear and rescued 'Tinker,' the hero of the contest, from his perilous position."

During the Civil War and in the years that followed, manufacturers developed more powerful guns. Until then only the bravest and most skillful hunters dared to face a full-grown grizzly. Now, with the new weapons, thousands of people decided that they were big-game hunters. They went into the forests and the hills to shoot wild animals, and the most prized trophy of all was the hide of a grizzly bear. This animal, which was the symbol of all that was wild and most fearsome in the Old West, began to disappear.

Grizzlies seldom bothered the farmers and ranchers anymore. The few that were left were learning to avoid human beings. They deserted their old haunts in the valleys and in the thickets along the streams. They retreated to the mountains.

More of the land became settled as new settlers poured into the West. Hunters entered every part of the wilderness. The large grizzly was left with no place to hide.

Grizzly Adams and a few other trappers captured grizzlies alive. As Adams discovered, these animals were too powerful and ferocious to tame like their close relatives, the brown bears of Europe, which had been tamed for centuries. So they were put in cages. A few of them lived on in zoos and circuses.

By the year 1900, the grizzly bear was simply a memory for a handful of old-timers in California. Its likeness appeared on the state flag, and it was the subject of many thrilling novels and histories about the region. But it was seldom seen in the wild anymore.

People went to the zoo in San Francisco's Golden Gate Park to see Monarch, which was the last California grizzly in captivity. He was very old, and in 1911 his keepers mercifully put him out of his misery.

Ten years later there were still occasional reports of a grizzly or two around Sequoia National Park. A hunter killed a grizzly near the park in 1922. People said they saw one in the vicinity two years later. And then there were no more reports.

The farmers and ranchers had decided that they could not live and raise crops and animals in a country that still held grizzly bears. California, Oregon, Washington, Arizona, and other states lost their bears. Even when hunters had killed most of them and driven the few survivors into the far wilderness, some people were not satisfied. The United States Government hired a staff of trappers to kill all wild animals that might destroy livestock. They pursued mountain lions, wolves, coyotes—and grizzly bears.

Aldo Leopold, America's most respected expert on wildlife, once wrote an essay about one of the last grizzlies in the Southwest. This bear lived on Escudilla, a wild and rugged mountain. Each spring the old grizzly crawled out of his den and came down the mountain. There he spent the rest of the year, peaceably feeding on berries, roots, and small animals.

Many states have lost their big bears. Alaska still has the brown bear, the largest of all and a close relative of the grizzly.

"No one ever saw the old bear," Leopold wrote, "but in the muddy springs about the base of the cliffs you saw his incredible tracks. Seeing them made the most hard-bitten cowboys aware of bear. Wherever they rode they saw the mountain, and when they saw the mountain they thought of bear."

Whether people lived exciting lives or boring ones, they knew that they lived in a special place. When they looked at Escudilla in the distance, they knew that it held a marvelous creature from another time. But one day a government trapper heard about the bear. He went into the mountain with his pack mule.

The trapper hunted the old bear on the mountain for many weeks, but he couldn't find him. He tried traps and poisons. The bear always escaped. Then the trapper found a path where the bear passed on the way to his den. He set up a gun in the path, with a string tied to the trigger. When the old bear passed that way, his foot hit the string and he shot himself.

"Escudilla still hangs on the horizon," Leopold wrote. "But when you see it you no longer think of bear. It's only a mountain now."

What Aldo Leopold meant was that human beings, in their eagerness to dominate their environment, had taken away something that was special. The same thing happened throughout most of the West.

4

BEGGAR BEARS

A curious event took place one evening at Yellowstone National Park. As dusk came on, groups of people gathered at the edge of a garbage dump near one of the park's hotels. Workers from the hotel began to unload containers of garbage onto the dump. As soon as they had left, a murmur of anticipation arose from the tourists who had gathered there.

As if on schedule, a black bear appeared out of the nearby trees and walked boldly onto the dump. It began to paw the mound and nibble at choice pieces of garbage. In a moment it was joined by a second black bear. Then another, and another.

A sudden yelp of excitement from one of the tourists drew everyone's attention back to the trees. In the shadows, watching the scene carefully, stood an enormous

Bears invaded the mounds of garbage behind the park's hotels.

figure. The words "grizzly bear" ran through the crowd. There were whispers of amazement and shudders of delicious fright.

The grizzly walked across the clearing toward the dump, stopping several times to look around and sniff the air. The black bears were dwarfed by the newcomer, which weighed over seven hundred pounds. They moved closer to the tourists, as if for protection, and fed on the leavings at the edge of the dump. The grizzly took the best place.

By the time darkness fell there were twenty black bears feeding on the dump. Three or four grizzlies could be seen behind them, moving around the garbage, and here and there finding something to their liking. The tourists stayed as long as they could make out even the faintest shadows of the big animals. Then they went back to their rooms in the hotel, satisfied that they had seen a show unlike anything else on earth.

But this was not an uncommon sight in Yellowstone National Park. It went on day after day, year after year. If a grizzly was seen in most places in the West, people either ran away from it or tried to kill it. In Yellowstone, the news that a wild grizzly could be seen brought people flocking there from all over the world. What had happened to bring about this difference in attitude?

The land around the Yellowstone River was passed by during the early settlement of the West. People rushed for gold in California, or for rich farmland in Washington and Oregon. The Yellowstone Valley was tucked away in the northern part of the Rocky Mountains. Only a few trappers had seen it. They came back to civilization with fantastic stories about a land where smoke and boiling water poured out of the earth to form a landscape of yellow rock and ghostly shapes.

In 1870 the United States Government sent an expedition to explore this mysterious land that was shut away from the path of human settlement. The members of the expedition discovered that the trappers were right. Hot springs bubbled in the earth. Geysers shot into the air, spraying water and steam as a volcano spews hot lava. The mineral-filled waters had carved the rocks into weird forms and stained them in yellow and other spectacular colors.

"It is grand, gloomy, and terrible," a member of the expedition wrote about the valley. "It is a solitude peopled with fantastic ideas—an empire of shadows and turmoil."

This mountainous land of lakes and rushing rivers and bubbling pools was not suitable for farming. As the explorers sat around their campfire in the evenings, they talked about the marvelous shapes they had seen there. They thought it would be a good idea if the government set aside this region so that all the people of the United States would be able to enjoy it.

When they returned to Washington, D.C., they told other people about their idea. The land they were so enthusiastic about lay in the northwest corner of Wyoming and included small parts of Montana and Idaho. Congress decided to create the first national park and call it Yellowstone after the brightly colored cliffs of the river that runs through it. At first Congress acted mainly to preserve the strange rock formations, the hot springs, and the geysers. But soon it was realized that this action would also protect the animals and plants that lived there.

Yet the federal government found it difficult to protect such a vast area. Hunters sneaked in and shot the elk, buffalo, and other large animals and sold their meat. Souvenir hunters and dealers in rare stones came to the park with sledgehammers and knocked down the rock formations so that they could cart them away and sell them in other parts of the country.

Finally, in 1886, the United States Cavalry was assigned to protect the park. Heavily armed soldiers rode out on horseback to guard this natural treasure.

The new railroads brought people from all over the

country to see this park and its wildlife. Hotels and restaurants were built in the park to house and feed the visitors.

The park became an ideal place in which to watch large wild animals. Bears, for instance, were abundant. They were there not because it was better "bear country" than any other place in the United States, but because most of the bears outside the park were being killed.

As visitors came to the park in increasing numbers, the hotels and restaurants were left with mounds of garbage. In this remote place there seemed nothing better to do with it than to haul it to dumps near the buildings.

Bears are alert, intelligent animals. They are able to change their habits to take advantage of a new situation. They quickly became aware that, at a certain time every evening, people brought loads of scraps and other garbage to those dumps. Like a dog that knows its owner will feed it at a certain time each day, the bears set their own inner "clocks" to the arrival of the garbagemen.

The tourists began to set their inner clocks too. They might have been interested in seeing a caged bear in a zoo or a circus. But how much more exciting it is to watch a wild grizzly step out of the forest in the gathering dusk. The word spread that wild bears could be seen at the dumps in the evening and the crowds gathered.

The U.S. Cavalry took no chances. An armed guard

stood at the dump in case there was trouble. In later years everyone treated this armed guard as a kind of joke.

"Are you here to protect us from the bears?" a visitor would ask the guard.

"No," the guard would always answer with a straight face. "I'm here to protect the *bears*."

But the situation in Yellowstone was not really a joke. The bears seemed to know that they were protected, and they became very bold. The tourists, on their part, began to think of these bears almost as pets. They thought the animals were cute and cuddly. They came closer and closer to the dumps while the bears were present.

"Of course, some adventurous souls took to hand-feeding the animals," wrote Paul Schullery in his book *The Bears of Yellowstone.* "It seemed only a matter of time before a bear would, literally, be fed a hand."

It was worse than that. In 1907 a foolish visitor to the park saw two grizzly cubs follow their mother to a dump. Playfully, the man chased the cubs. When the frightened animals climbed a tree, he poked at them with his umbrella. The enraged mother grizzly killed the man.

The park authorities forbade the public to feed or otherwise disturb the animals, but many people paid no attention to the rules. When a black bear or a grizzly saw a human being, it thought only of being fed. As more and more people began to camp in tents inside the park, bears learned that the campgrounds were another source of food. They entered the campgrounds at night to rip open bags and boxes in their search. Sometimes they invaded tents. They never learned to say "Please."

Congress created the National Park Service in 1916 to operate Yellowstone and other parks that had come into existence around the country. Park rangers replaced soldiers in the parks. The new Park Service was eager to increase the number of visitors. If more people came to the parks, Congress would provide more money for their "development."

A little over 25,000 people visited Yellowstone in 1916, but a few years later more than ten times that number came. A great many of them came to watch bears. For that reason, the park authorities did not always enforce the rules about feeding animals.

The development of the automobile made it much easier for people to reach this remote park. Modern roads were built to carry the traffic. Soon "beggar bears" began to line the roads in the park. One of these bears grew so fearless about stopping cars for a handout that he became known as "Jesse James."

When Yellowstone's bears saw human beings, they began to think of being fed.

If a bear was seen along the road, all the cars would stop. People would get out to feed the bears or take their pictures. Traffic jams became a part of this wild country —rangers called them "bear jams."

If tourists did not have food with them, they offered the bear almost anything, from candy wrappers to bottle tops. The bears, smelling something interesting, often swallowed those objects.

Around the bears people acted in the most stupid manner possible. They pushed their children toward the wild animals to get pictures of child and bear standing together. Some people spread jelly on their children's arms to get pictures of a bear licking it off!

"Do you mean to tell me those cute creatures will harm anyone?" a tourist said after being warned by a ranger. "Why, they smile and wiggle their tails in the most cunning manner!"

"Yes," the ranger replied, "but you must not trust either end of a bear."

Every year many visitors were injured. Sometimes, when a person handed a bit of food to a bear, the animal wanted the rest of it. The person tried to close the bag of food, but the hungry bear simply took what it wanted, and the visitor went off to the hospital.

As injuries increased, park officials tried once more to control the feeding of bears. Rangers gave stern warnings to people who were gathering around a bear. New methods were found to remove "problem bears." A special gun was developed to fire a dart that drugged a bear but did not injure it. Rangers then took the bear far into the wilderness, away from people and cars. Many of the garbage dumps in the park were closed. If a bear kept coming back and became dangerous, the rangers had to shoot it.

Rangers also tried to reason with people. They pointed out that many of the objects fed to bears were harmful to them. Even healthy foods simply kept bears around until trouble began. Paul Schullery, who was a ranger-naturalist in the park, saw some of the worst problems.

"Some visitors are not at all concerned about the condition of the bear," he wrote. "They want only the chance to see it. I once explained to an apparently intelligent visitor that during the 1960s an average of twenty-four black bears were destroyed every year because of troubles with begging. The visitor's response was that it was worth it. He said that was a reasonable price to pay, so that he could see bears. Fortunately this sickness of mind is not common."

Garbage dumps, however, remained a favorite gathering place for both bears and people. Up to seventy black bears and grizzlies could be seen feeding at one time. But many people were beginning to realize that they were seriously changing the habits of Yellowstone's bears. Some of these bears were no longer wild animals. They were simply beggars who had become dependent on handouts.

A group of scientists made a study of the problem. They agreed that the park was a place where animals should be preserved in their wild state. By attracting these animals to dumps, human beings were destroying their wildness.

"The sight of one bear in the forest," the scientists wrote, "is more exciting than a close association with dozens of bears at a dump."

The argument about bears was just beginning.

5

A SUCCESSFUL ANIMAL

A car pulled off the road in the rural section of a far northern state. A man, a woman, and two children got out and walked into a field, carrying small metal containers. They began to pick wild blueberries. Suddenly one of the children jumped up excitedly.

"Look!" she called, pointing across the field. "There's a bear!"

For a moment the others thought she was joking. But then they looked to where the child was pointing. And there, standing on its hind legs, staring in their direction and sniffing the air, was a black bear. In a flash it dropped to all fours and disappeared into the tall bushes at the edge of the field.

None of the four people would ever forget that late summer day. It was the first bear they had ever seen in the wild. For years afterward they would tell their friends and relatives about that exciting moment when they discovered they were sharing a field of berries with a bear.

A scene such as this is not unusual in parts of North America today. The black bear lives throughout much of the United States and Canada—north, south, east, and west. No other kind of bear is so successful in finding ways to go on living in a world where human beings try to make all the rules.

The black bear, as we have seen, is not as large or as fierce as the grizzly. That is one reason why it has been able to live near towns and villages. Human beings have not felt the need to wipe out this animal, as they have destroyed the grizzly. But, in its own way, the black bear is as interesting in its environment as any animal on earth.

People are often surprised to discover that black bears live in their vicinity. As long as there is a large forest nearby, bears are likely to be present. They do not always keep to the deep woods. One reason that bears are seldom seen in the wild by human beings is that they are always on the move. They do not wander aimlessly. They move about without hurry, constantly looking for food, poking their noses into rotting stumps or under old logs or into thick berry bushes.

People who spend much time in the woods and fields are fortunate because they have a chance to watch bears in their own
environment.

Black bears live in the forest community of North America. This is a community of many different kinds of plants and animals, and many different kinds of feeding places. The bears roam from one kind of place to another, from the deep forests to the banks of swift-flowing streams, and from steep mountainsides to open fields where berries and juicy grasses grow. Bears are always pushing at the edges of their world.

People who spend much of their time in the woods and fields are the fortunate ones. They have an opportunity to watch black bears in their environment. They begin to know, after years of patient watching, a little bit about how bears live.

Black bears are not often thought of as beautiful animals. Yet there is a certain grace and beauty in the way they move through their environment. They are sturdy, almost roly-poly at times, but their actions can be swift and agile if the need arises. Let us take a close look at one of them as it steps out of the forest into the sunlight on the meadow's edge.

The black bear is not always black. Its thick fur may be very dark in the eastern United States, but in the West the color ranges from brown to nearly blond. Even if it is a male, the black bear probably weighs no more than 250 pounds, and on all fours it stands less than thirty-two inches at the shoulder. A female is noticeably smaller.

The bear's frame, or skeleton, gives it many advantages over other animals. The skeleton is large and very sturdy, yet it also allows the bear great freedom of movement. The bones of the legs are separate, like those in human beings. A bear is able to turn its front legs and paws easily, just as we turn our arms and hands, and so it develops great skill in digging, handling food, and performing other useful actions.

Bears perform many actions as apes or humans do. They sit upright with their legs stretched out in front of them. At those times they remind us of some hairy giant, sitting peacefully in the shade of an old tree.

The bear's snout is short, ending in a piglike nose that is very useful to the bear because it is amazingly sensitive to odors. It enables the animal to sniff out hidden food or to discover an enemy who may be some distance away.

This ability is important to the bear. Its small eyes are nearsighted, so the nose helps it to make sense of distant objects when the eyes cannot focus on them. The eyes are of most service up close, helping the bear to find the ants and other small objects it often feeds on. But the small ears are extremely sensitive instruments. They are able to pick up sounds that a human being cannot hear.

If a bear's head seems small, its neck is enormous. It is

packed in layers of powerful muscles. Some of those muscles control the animal's big jaws, while others are attached to the upper front legs and shoulders.

Most of the large mammals with which we are familiar in North America have slender legs and walk on hoofs, like horses and deer, or on the tips of their toes, like dogs and cats. A bear walks on the entire bottom of its feet, just as human beings do.

The feet of the bear are large and flat. They are protected by a thick pad across the palm and smaller pads on each of the five toes. A bear's big toe is on the outside of its foot.

Each toe also has a strong claw, which may be an inch or more long. The claws on the front feet are curved. They are useful tools for digging in the ground or in rotten logs and for handling objects that the bear wants to pick up.

The back claws are straight and help the black bear to climb trees. As a rule, the cubs climb more easily than adults. The animals dig their claws into the trunk of a tree, which gives them a firm foothold. Scientists are able to look at an aspen or other tree with smooth bark and

---

The claws on the hind feet of a black bear are straight, helping it to climb trees. Cubs climb more easily than adults.

47

tell that a bear climbed it, perhaps several years earlier. The claws leave telltale marks in the bark, which are then covered by prominent scabs.

A wild bear seldom walks around on its hind legs, as a trained bear does in the circus. But when it does stand erect, it balances itself easily on its large, flat feet. It stands mostly to look around in tall grass or bushes, or perhaps to come to blows with another bear. The bear also stands upright to gather fruits or nuts from the overhanging bushes or trees.

The forest in which the bear lives is full of nourishing things to eat, and the black bear is well equipped to make use of them. With its agile front legs and strong curved claws, it can rip juicy plants from the earth or dig out insects from a dead tree. With its keen nose it can sniff out sweets such as honey in a beehive, depending on its dense fur to protect it from the angry bees.

Scientists call the black bear an *omnivore*, which means that it eats almost anything. Nature has fitted this animal to make use of whatever it finds in the forest. It has powerful jaws and a set of forty-two teeth of different kinds. Some of the teeth are broad and almost flat, designed for crushing nuts or other hard objects. Other teeth are long and sharp, good for tearing the flesh of the animals it eats.

The black bear is a successful animal in nature's terms,

having few enemies in the forest community in which it lives. Its size, its quickness, and its keen senses fit it to make use of a wide variety of foods. The black bear may live for fifteen years or more in the wild. In captivity it may live twice that long.

One certain sign of the black bear's resourcefulness is that there are so many of its kind left in North America, in spite of long persecution by humans. Most hunters believe that a bear is the finest prize to be found in the forest. Naturalist and writer Ernest Thompson Seton described some famous bear hunters of the American past. A hunter in New York killed ninety-six black bears in three years. Another in Pennsylvania killed four hundred in his lifetime. Even today, in a densely forested state such as Maine, this species has been wiped out in the heavily populated counties.

After we have heard stories like that, we find it hard to believe that black bears remain plentiful in modern times. But, in 1953, seven hundred were killed in Canada just to supply bearskin hats for the Brigade of Guards at the coronation of Great Britain's Queen Elizabeth II.

"Fortunately for the black bear," someone wrote at the time, "Great Britain's coronations are not frequent."

6

THE YEAR OF THE BEAR

I SPRING

Poets often write that spring is an awakening. Bears in northern lands are a part of this vast natural event.

A bear meets the spring sleepily. It climbs slowly from the den where it has spent the winter months, not in a deep sleep, but curled up and dozing on and off. It is not yet fully alert.

As the bear steps into the spring sunlight, it does not appear very different from the animal that went into the den the previous fall. But it has lost a great deal of weight, perhaps as much as one-fourth of what it weighed a few months earlier. It will lose even more weight during the first few weeks after it leaves the den.

Fortunately for the bear, it is not very hungry when

it comes out of the den. It is still living on the body fat it built up the year before. There is not much to eat in the northern countryside during early spring. The bear finds mostly winter's leftovers—dead grass and a few roots that it is able to dig from the thawing earth.

But sometimes there is more. Winter can be very hard on the other animals in the forest community that do not hibernate—or go into a den to sleep—as the bear does. Many deer, moose, elk, and other animals die of hunger or disease. Young animals that are born in early spring may also die if the weather is harsh. The bear, which is very sensitive to odors in the forest, may discover the carcass of one of those unfortunate animals and enjoy an easy meal.

The bear becomes more alert as the weather grows warmer. Its hunger increases. If it has no cubs, it probably wanders more at this time of year than it will later on because food is still scarce. It travels alone, for bears do not usually cluster in large numbers except under special conditions—as at a garbage dump, or when a favorite food such as berries or fish is concentrated at one point.

The bear does a lot of digging in the ground. It is mainly after roots, which store much nourishment. Adolph Murie, a naturalist who studied bears in Alaska, often watched them at work.

"To get at the roots," Murie wrote, "the bear usually places both paws on the ground and thrusts back with the body until a chunk of soil is loosened. This is turned over and the free roots are eaten. Then, with a paw working slowly and lightly, more of the tender roots are uncovered and eaten. The fleshy roots were up to a half-inch thick and looked like dandelion roots."

Bears also like wild onions. Once in a while a bear discovers a rodent in the ground, which it will kill and eat.

The grizzly is an expert at fishing. It wades into the shallow water and catches fish with a swipe of its paw. The black bear does not seem to have the patience to wait for a long time until a fish comes along, but it will take a dead or dying fish along the shore.

Bears also eat the rich, tender layer of trees called *cambium*. Adolph Murie's brother, Olaus, described bears biting and pulling off strips of bark from the trunks of evergreen trees to get at the cambium.

"Having pulled away the bark," Olaus Murie wrote, "they will scrape off the juicy substance on the wood with their teeth, leaving tooth marks. I tasted some of this. At first there was syrupy sweetness, followed at once by turpentine! But the bears like it."

In spring the lone bear wanders far in search of something besides food. It is looking for a mate. Some bears are ready to mate by the fourth summer of their lives, but in most cases the female is not ready until her fifth summer.

The bear, which we are likely to think of as an old grouch living by itself, is an entirely different animal during the mating season in late spring and early summer. It wants a companion and searches until it finds one. Even if the female is not ready to mate for several weeks, the two bears usually travel together very peaceably. Adolph Murie watched a couple of grizzlies.

"They were together most of the time and were often playing and hugging," Murie wrote. "They wrestled, then fed close together on roots. Later they wrestled again. The male grabbed the female with his jaws back of an ear and tried to mount her, but she rolled over. They continued to wrestle and play for some time, then went back to feeding on roots."

When the female is ready, the two bears mate. They remain together for several more weeks, mating and feeding. It is important for the female to spend much of the time feeding, for she will soon be pregnant and need the extra nourishment.

The mating season ends suddenly. The two bears lose interest in each other, and the male goes away. He will play no further part in caring for the family he has helped to start.

II SUMMER

Each bear is alone once more. Whether it is a black bear or a grizzly, it is mainly a vegetarian. Perhaps four-fifths of its diet is made up of plants and their nuts and fruits.

Bears eat many kinds of grasses, but berries are a special treat. If berries are plentiful in a certain field, the bear may abandon its usual solitary habits and join other bears in gathering the rich harvest. In that case the biggest and strongest bear will seize the best berry patch for itself.

The bear likes all kinds of berries. It eats strawberries, serviceberries, raspberries, and choke cherries. A bear that is in a berry patch is not a picky eater. It grabs a branch with a paw and pulls it to its mouth. Leaves and twigs go down into its huge stomach along with the berries.

In Maine a good place to see a bear is in the blueberry fields. The growers put out hives of bees in early summer to pollinate the blueberry blossoms, and the bear comes to steal the honey from the hives. When the berries ripen, the bear returns for another meal.

As we know, a bear is not always a vegetarian. Animals are eaten also, and no animal is too small to interest even a very large bear. Paul Schullery described how a bear feeds at an ant hill.

"Early naturalists claimed that the bear, on discovering an ant hill, would remove its top, stick its nose into the center tunnel, and inhale the ants," Schullery wrote. "The real approach is much more practical. A quick swipe of the paw wrecks the hill, and the paw is then laid in the center of the struggling insects. Once a sufficient number of ants have swarmed onto the paw to 'defend' their home, the bear licks them off."

A bear seems to like the sharp, acid taste of ants. It also searches the grass for grasshoppers and crickets and turns over rocks for mice. When it stops at a pond to drink, it may pick up a frog or salamander. Adolph Murie told of how a bear, with her three cubs nearby, hunted ground squirrels. She had dug a trench fifteen feet long, tearing out the sod, or chunks of earth.

"The mother would place both front paws on the sod and push downward and pull back until the piece gave way," Murie wrote. "Sometimes the bear seemed to push down on the sod to scare the squirrel and make it come out. She would paw out the dirt and take frequent sniffs at the mouth of the hole where she was working. Once she reached into the hole with her arm, lying on her side so she could reach in farther."

But the bear could not reach the little animal. So she

No animal is too small to interest a bear. It will eat grasshoppers and even ants.

went to another place and pressed down the sod with her front paws to loosen it. Suddenly the squirrel scurried out of the hole.

"The bear jumped for it," Murie wrote. "But the squirrel dodged to one side and managed to escape from four pounces. The last time it left the bear flatfooted off to one side. But with the next pounce the bear captured the squirrel. The cubs sat close by, watching the mother chew the squirrel, but she made no offer to share it with them. One cub did get a piece which dropped from her jaws."

Summer is a lazy time for a lone bear. Some bears, especially black bears, feed much of the time at night. If a bear feeds during the day, it may rest, or "shade up," when the sun is very warm. It may even scrape together a daytime bed of leaves or branches and take a nap in the shade.

A sure sign that a bear spends time in an area is the appearance of a "bear tree." This is a tree that shows the marks made by a bear. Perhaps there is a place on the trunk where the bark has been ripped away and toothmarks left in the wood. Or perhaps there are scars left by a young black bear's claws as it climbed into the branches.

But a bear will use a favorite tree for another purpose.

"Bears like to rub themselves on a tree," Olaus Murie

wrote. "They will rub and rub, sometimes grasping the tree and clawing it, sometimes biting it as they stand on their hind legs. Often this tree is in a prominent place, on a point or beside the trail, where it easily comes to the notice of the bear. It is rubbed and scratched repeatedly until we recognize it as an established 'bear tree.' Generally, pitch oozes out and you will find hairs stuck in it, or clinging to the bark."

III FALL

The days of a northern bear take on a more urgent tone as fall advances. Life will not become so different in the colder months for bears in the southern United States because they do not have to hibernate. But snow and ice are coming, the northern bear's instinct tells it, and it must begin to prepare for them.

Fall brings a new harvest. There are acorns and other nuts for bears to feed on. Standing on its hind legs, a bear can reach nuts and fruit that are ten feet or more above the ground. The smaller black bear holds an advantage over a grizzly in this case. It is able to climb up into a tree to gather food that is beyond its reach. The grizzly, which does not climb trees, must be content to feed on the lower branches.

The bear still digs for roots and rodents in this season.

Fall brings a new harvest. There are nuts and berries for bears to feed on.

If it is lucky, it may gain another benefit from digging. Squirrels, mice, and other rodents are busily preparing for the winter too, hiding away nuts and other food. If a bear finds this small treasure, it will make short work of it.

As a rule, a bear cannot chase fleet-footed animals such as deer or antelope with much success. If it kills one, the chances are that the victim was already sick or injured. But if heavy snow falls before the bear goes into hibernation, it may kill a large animal that is bogged down in the snow.

Glen Cole, a biologist with the National Park Service, described how a grizzly kills a large animal.

"Bears pulled down running elk by rearing on their hind legs and grasping an animal on or over the rump," Cole wrote. "They apparently allowed their weight to collapse the elk's hindquarters. Bears then grabbed and vigorously shook the elk's neck with their jaws. They rolled the elk over on its back, and opened the abdomen. The neck was grabbed and shaken again if the elk continued to struggle."

Early snow may bring an easier kill. Tiny flying insects often rest on snowbanks, where they are seen by a bear. The large animal simply sticks out its tongue and licks them off.

The bear eats at a furious rate. During the fall months

it may gain a pound or more a day. Layers of fat—sometimes four inches thick!—grow around its body. This fat will go on providing the animal with energy after it has stopped feeding and goes into hibernation. Fat also provides the bear with insulation against the cold.

Fall advances toward winter. Food grows scarce in the northern land. The bear prowls the forest and protected hillsides, looking for a good place to spend the winter. It does not need a broad, roomy cave. Snugness is important. It looks for a hole in a hillside or under the roots of a fallen tree, just large enough to hold its curled-up body. With its tough claws it enlarges the den and shapes the space to its own needs.

The bear works on its den just as a bird works at building its nest. Bears seem to learn by experience, because older ones are likely to choose more suitable sites. Under the roots of a fallen tree is usually a good choice for a den because the roots, anchored in the ground, give the den some sturdiness, just as timbers support a house. Grass, moss, and evergreen boughs are carried inside to line the den.

Usually the first bear to go into hibernation is the pregnant female. The pregnancy is perfectly timed with the period of hibernation. Almost as soon as pregnancy began in early summer, the embryo stopped developing. It grew hardly at all during the summer and early fall.

Only now, when the cold weather of late fall arrives, does the embryo begin to grow again. The embryo is still hardly the size of a speck.

The temperature falls and dark clouds gather in the sky. Snow begins falling. The bear, almost roly-poly in its thick layers of fat, its belly almost dragging the ground, makes its way through the dusk to the hillside it already knows so well. It squeezes through the network of roots that cover the opening like the bars of a gate.

The snow falls all that night and the wind piles it in deep drifts on the hillside. When morning comes, the den's opening has disappeared under the great white blanket.

IV WINTER

The den of the hibernating bear would seem almost like a tomb to anyone who was given a chance to glance inside. Deep under the snow, and rolled up in its layers of fat, the bear hardly looks like a living creature. Its temperature has dropped, its heartbeat has slowed down. The woody materials it has eaten just before hibernating form a plug that allows nothing to leave its digestive tract.

"The undisturbed Yellowstone black bear sleeps without eating, drinking, or passing any substance through its system, for four or five months," Paul Schullery wrote. "This is the equivalent of getting up from Thanksgiving

dinner and taking a nap until Easter. And maybe giving birth in the meantime. We must be impressed, if not awed, by such an achievement."

Yet life goes on in the den. Life is growing, if only very slowly, inside the pregnant female. If this is her first pregnancy, the bear probably is carrying only one cub. If she is a more experienced mother, she may give birth to two or three cubs.

Many centuries ago, shortly after the birth of Christ, a Roman citizen named Pliny wrote a book about natural history. Very few scientific studies had been made on the lives of animals at that time, and many of the things Pliny wrote about them just are not true.

"Bears when first born are shapeless masses of white flesh," Pliny wrote. "They are little larger than mice. The mother then licks them gradually into proper shape."

It is easy to understand why people believed this. Bears are curious-looking little creatures when they are born, no larger than a squirrel. But this tininess is an advantage to animals that are born during their mother's hibernation. If they were born any larger, they would quickly drain the food that is stored in her body. That food must

---

Deep under the snow, and rolled up in its layers of fat, the black bear in hibernation hardly looks like a living creature.

last until she leaves the den and finds a plentiful supply in the spring.

The cubs are born blind and hairless. But they are able to find their mother's nipples in the dark and begin sucking milk. The mother goes on dozing, though she must be aware that the cubs are nearby. If not she might roll over and crush them.

Outside the den the days are growing longer. Periods of warm sun are melting the deep snow cover. The bear and her cubs begin to stir in the den.

One day the old bear squeezes through the roots at the opening, pushes aside the remaining snow, and walks sleepily into the sunlight. Three cubs climb out behind her. They weigh about five pounds each and wobble on their short, unsteady legs. Each of the cubs may have grown fur of a different color.

"I saw a bear and her three cubs," an elderly miner once told Adolph Murie. "There was one lemon, one orange, and a chocolate!"

Until recent years we did not know much more about bears and their family lives than Pliny did. A few scientists have helped to change that. Their careful and sometimes dangerous work, as we shall see, has increased our knowledge about these sensitive, intelligent animals.

The bears that follow their mother from the den are playful animals.

7
THE STUDY TEAM

I

Beep! Beep! Beep!

Three men were gathered around a small radio receiver overlooking a valley in Yellowstone National Park. It was fall, and snow flurries were in the air.

Beep! Beep! Beep!

The excitement of the men increased as they listened to the signal on their receiver. It came in loud and clear.

"We could hear the howling of coyotes and the challenging bugle of bull elk," Frank Craighead wrote. "Canada geese honked upriver. But the metallic sound we were listening to had nothing of wildness about it. No deep primitive instinct of the chase stirred in us at the sound. Yet this beeping coming to us in the vastness of Hayden Valley thrilled us as few sounds ever had."

Frank Craighead and his twin brother, John, were the leaders of a team that was beginning the most complete study ever made on the grizzly bear. The sound they heard on their receiver came from a tiny radio attached to a wild grizzly that was roaming somewhere in the valley below. By following these sounds, the Craigheads and a student assistant hoped to learn the secrets of a grizzly's life.

Until they began their study, the story of the grizzly had been a jumble of fact and fiction. It was based largely on the tales of hunters, who were not always reliable. Scientific facts were added little by little, sometimes by accident. No one had followed individual bears throughout the year, and from one year to another. No one had put the whole story together.

Frank and John Craighead were well qualified to make this study. When they were teenagers, *National Geographic* published an article about their adventures with birds of prey called falcons. The brothers went on to study wildlife all over the world. Their articles and films told millions of people about animals. Now, through an agreement with the National Park Service, they were trying to understand the lives of Yellowstone's grizzlies.

Beep! Beep! Beep!

The brothers set off across the valley with their assistant. The high-pitched sounds coming in on their receiver reminded them of all the work that had been done, and of all the money that had been spent on equipment, to bring them to this point. But most of all their minds were on the bear that was moving through the trees ahead of them. It was a sow, or female grizzly, that they had named Marian.

The Craigheads had two goals in mind in making this study. They wanted to increase humanity's knowledge about these animals. They also wanted to put this knowledge to use in preserving the last population of grizzlies in the lower forty-eight United States. The California grizzly had disappeared almost before anyone realized what had happened. The Craigheads did not want that to happen to Yellowstone's bears.

How large is this population? How far does it roam? Is the population growing larger or smaller? How do the bears live in winter? What happens to the cubs after they leave the den? Much of what we know about grizzlies today came from the lengthy study that the Craigheads began in 1959.

There is a great difference between studying an animal in a laboratory or zoo and studying one in the wild. The grizzly presents special problems. It roams over many miles of rough country. It is usually secretive and solitary in its habits. It is a dangerous animal if approached closely.

Some of the Craigheads' equipment had been familiar to biologists for many years. They carried maps and notebooks and binoculars. In winter they traveled through Yellowstone's back country on skis. But they also needed space-age tools. They asked other scientists to develop small, durable radios that could be attached to bears. By following the *beeps*, or signals, sent out constantly by those radios, the Craigheads would be able to keep track of the bears.

How does a biologist get a wild grizzly to carry a radio? The Craigheads found a way. They built a culvert trap. It was made of a large metal cylinder, similar to the culverts, or pipes, that carry water under a road. To one end of the trap they fixed a heavy door that could be raised and lowered on a cable. They closed off the other end.

The Craigheads mounted the trap on a trailer and pulled it to an area where they had seen grizzlies feeding. They left meat in the trap, tied to the cable that held the door open. When a bear climbed into the trap to get the meat, the cable broke loose and the door slammed shut.

The next morning the Craigheads found a grizzly in their trap. When Frank Craighead looked inside, the angry bear struck at him with a paw. He leaped back just in time to escape being clawed. He raised his rifle

The biologists built a culvert trap. To one end they fixed a heavy door that could be raised and lowered on a cable.

and fired a dart into the animal's neck. The tip of the dart carried a powerful drug that quickly put the bear to sleep. Then the study team opened the door and pulled the drugged bear out of the cage.

The biologists discovered it was a female. After lifting her onto a set of scales with the aid of a pulley and a stout rope net, they learned that she weighed three hundred pounds. They measured her and took dental casts and a blood sample. The condition of the teeth would help to tell the Craigheads how old the bear was—this one was about three and a half years old, they discovered. The blood sample helped them decide if she was healthy.

The grizzly stirred and coughed. The men knew they had to work fast. They put batteries into the small radio, which was waterproofed and built to stand hard knocks. They made sure the instrument was tightly fastened to a sturdy collar, then they slipped the collar around the bear's neck.

The bear lifted her head. She was beginning to shake off the effects of the drug.

"Let's get out of here," Frank Craighead shouted to the others.

They ran off and took a position on higher ground. As they watched, the bear they called Marian got to her feet. She shook her head, looked around, and walked off into the forest. Frank Craighead snapped on the radio receiver. The members of the study team smiled happily when they heard the signal sent out by the radio that was carried through the forest by Marian.

This was the first free-roaming grizzly ever tracked by radio. During the next two years of their study the Craigheads captured sixty-seven bears. They marked each of them with colored ear tags so that they could tell one bear from another at a distance. They put a radio collar on each of them. Then, as long as each animal lived, the biologists kept careful records of its age, feeding habits, and health. They kept track of where it wandered and how many cubs it raised during its lifetime.

When the batteries in a radio collar began to fade, the Craigheads recaptured the bear. Sometimes they caught it in the culvert trap, sometimes they shot it in the open meadows with a dart gun. By recapturing a bear, they were also able to study its physical changes.

The brothers gave each bear a different number. Many of these bears, however, had some physical mark that distinguished them even without their numbers and color tags. The brothers made up names for these familiar individuals—Scarface, Cutlip, Pegleg, Lover Boy, Rip-nosed Sow, and Notch Ear. They called one young grizzly

They snapped a radio collar on Marian and fastened colored
tags to her ears.

the Sucostrin Kid because it took a large dose of the drug Sucostrin to knock him out.

II

This last population of grizzlies in the United States south of Alaska lives in the mountain country and wilderness forests of Montana, Idaho, and Wyoming. The Craigheads' study revealed that there were perhaps six or seven hundred grizzlies in the region. As the years passed, they became familiar with many of these animals. Day after day they followed the series of beeps that led them to a bear. They had many adventures as they kept track of whole families of bears in the magnificent Yellowstone back country.

"We continued to follow the family after they entered a rocky ravine," Frank Craighead wrote in his exciting book, *Track of the Grizzly.* "It was an area of thermal activity with small, constantly playing geysers, rising steam, hot springs, small mud pots, and boggy areas of doubtful footing. It was a natural greenhouse with ample food for bears, but to us it possessed an air of mystery and even gloom. The changing density of the moving mist generated by the cooling afternoon air caused objects to fade, then disappear. The steam from hotter thermal waters contributed to the ghostly atmosphere. When we emerged into the timber from the gorge, we nearly ran into three grizzlies."

During more than ten years of studying the bears, the Craigheads always carried a gun, but they never had to use it. When the three grizzlies appeared in front of them on this day, there were tall trees nearby. The men moved close to the trees, ready to climb if the bears attacked. But, as the brothers had learned, most grizzlies prefer to avoid humans who do not threaten them. The grizzlies turned and went their own way.

The bear the brothers knew best was Marian, the young sow that carried their first radio collar. But even Marian gave them some anxious moments. When following a bear through the forest, they usually were able to tell how close they were to it by the strength of the radio signal. A loud *beep* warned them that a bear was close by. One day when they were following Marian the signal faded. They guessed that she was moving rapidly away from them, so they began to hurry after her.

"Suddenly the signal boomed out loud and clear, an indication that the bear was dangerously close," Frank Craighead wrote. "Marian suddenly rose up from her day bed and glared at us from only forty feet away. A larger, more aggressive bear would almost surely have charged us if we had jumped it in this manner. Marian appeared to be even more surprised than we were. She sprinted away."

After he calmed down, Frank Craighead figured out what had happened. Marian wanted to take a nap. She dug out a resting place at the base of a fallen tree. When she lay down, the thick network of roots partly blocked the signals from her radio. So the signal fooled the men, sounding to them as if it were coming from a long distance.

The Craigheads followed Marian to her den every year. When she left in the spring, they crawled inside the snug chamber and noted how she had arranged her bed of evergreen boughs. They wondered how warm it remained in the den under the thick blanket of snow.

That summer they captured Marian again and put a new instrument on her radio collar. The speed at which the signals sounded now would tell the listeners aboveground what the temperature was in the den. The roof of her old den had recently fallen in, covering the floor with mud. In the fall the brothers watched her dig out and prepare a den in another hillside.

They followed her closely that fall. The den was ready, but Marian wandered widely. She was pregnant and seemed to know that she must gather extra nourishment for the months ahead.

One day the skies clouded over. Marian headed straight for her den. Shortly before she arrived it began to snow very hard. Marian entered the den, and by morning the snow had completely covered the opening, as well as her tracks. Like other bears, her amazing sensitivity to weather conditions sent her into hibernation at just the right moment.

During the winter the Craigheads, with the aid of radio signals, checked the temperatures in the dens of Marian and other bears. For instance, the temperature in one den remained at a steady level of 26° to 28° Fahrenheit, while outside it rose and fell many degrees. The bear remained warm under the layers of fat and fur.

Marian gave birth to two cubs that winter. In the spring they followed her out of the den into their bright new world. For some days the cubs played and rested near the den, while the Craigheads watched the family from a distance. They saw Marian, half sitting, half lying on her back, as she nursed her cubs.

"When she tired of nursing," Frank Craighead wrote, "she cuffed her youngsters aside, rose to her feet, then rolled over first one, then the other, with a gentle sweep of her powerful paw. This was all the energetic cubs needed to start a wrestling match, rolling, running, cuffing, and growling. Sometimes they wrestled with their mother, sometimes each other. Occasionally all three were part of a confused jumble out of which a cub would dart, then turn and scamper back for more buffeting.

"As usual, the mother tired first and started moving away, only to be attacked by her tireless cubs. A sharp cuff that knocked both of them over ended the play and reminded the cubs that obedience was necessary and demanded by all mother bears. Disobedience when danger threatened could well mean death."

That year the Craigheads watched the cubs follow their mother to the feeding areas. She tended them closely. If one wandered away, she would run after it, cuffing it to make it obey. In late fall she dug out another den and took the cubs inside with her for the winter.

When another spring rolled around, the plump cubs were old enough to care for themselves. Marian drove them away. A young bear seldom likes to be sent off on its own, and often a severe beating by the mother is necessary to finally send it packing. Then Marian found a mate and began a new family.

III

During the years that the Craigheads carried on their study, there were important changes in Yellowstone

National Park. The park's officials decided that they must do everything possible to make the bears of Yellowstone completely wild once more. They closed the last of the garbage dumps. They believed the Craigheads' study should come to an end. But the information gained by the study team would help other biologists for years to come.

One of the unfortunate victims of the new policy was Marian. Like other Yellowstone bears, she sometimes visited the garbage dumps for food. One day, after the last dump was closed, she and her cub entered a campground to look for an easy meal.

A ranger was called by frightened campers. He shot the cub with a drug-tipped dart. Then he moved toward the cub, planning to take it to one of the park's wild areas. But Marian thought the ranger was going to harm the cub. When she rushed him, he put a bullet between her eyes.

Marian's death proved that the problems between humans and bears had not yet been solved. The park's officials had changed the rules. But the bears were not able to read the new regulations, and they went on behaving as people had encouraged them to, returning to places where they had always found food before. Many bears would be killed before they learned the new rules.

But a beginning had been made. Gathering information

about wild animals is the first step in preserving them. The next step is for biologists and government officials to come together and use the information to make wise decisions. Only then will the mistakes of the past be avoided.

8

BEARS AROUND THE WORLD

I

Every two years scientists from many countries gather in a city somewhere in Europe to talk about polar bears. They pool their information—that is, each scientist lets the others know what he or she has learned about polar bears since the last meeting.

Polar bears live at the top of the world. They are not the problem of just one or two countries, in the way that saving grizzly bears is a problem for the United States and Canada. Five important nations—the United States, Canada, the Soviet Union, Norway, and Denmark, which owns Greenland—all control land around the Arctic ice where polar bears roam. Each of these nations must find solutions to the problems that are faced by this endangered species.

Scientific meetings to discuss the world's bears are

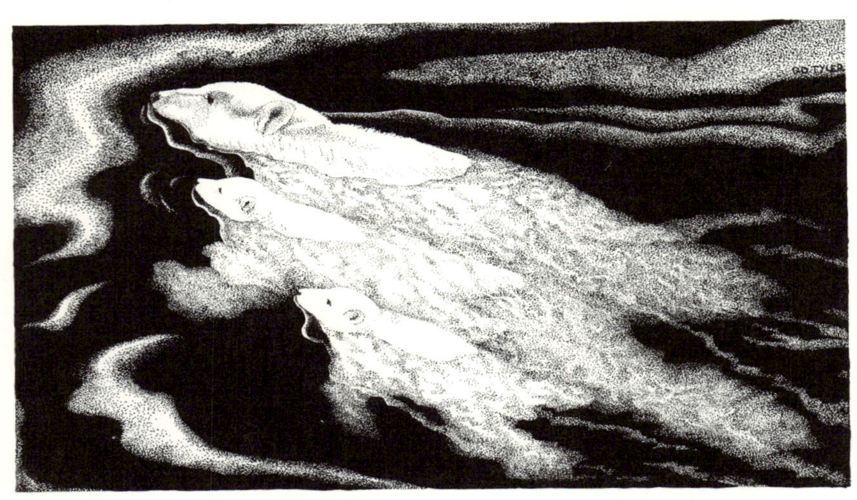

Polar bears live at the top of the world. Here a mother and her two cubs swim toward an ice floe.

becoming very common today. Bears used to live all across Europe, Asia, and North America. Only the black bear of North America has partly managed to hold its own. The other kinds of bears have disappeared from many of the places where they once lived. In the places where they still exist they are in trouble.

Scientists such as Frank and John Craighead have learned much about grizzlies in recent years. But hardly anything is known about some of the other kinds of bears that live in other parts of the world. How many bears are there of each kind? How much forest or other wild land do they need in order to survive? If scientists are going to help them, they will need to know the answers to questions like these.

II

The brown bears are more widespread than any other member of this animal family. For thousands of years they were the only ones that most people in Europe and Asia knew anything about. Centuries ago they were found all the way from Great Britain to Japan, and then across to western North America. They lived southward to the Mediterranean Sea and the Himalayas.

Until recent years even scientists were not aware that

brown bears in western Europe belonged to the same species as the brown bears in eastern Asia and North America. Individual bears in one region often differ a great deal in size and color from those in another region. For instance, some brown bears that live in Syria weigh only about 150 pounds. But brown bears that live in Alaska may weigh ten times as much!

So there was much confusion. Scientists in Europe said there were at least six species, or kinds, of brown bears. In North America one famous scientist decided there were eighty-six different kinds of grizzlies and brown bears. But in recent years many close studies have been made of these animals' skeletons and other physical characteristics. When a male and a female of this species are brought together, even if they come from widely separated parts of the world, they are able to mate and produce young. Nearly everyone agrees now that all the brown bears make up a single species.

European people always marveled at the size and strength of brown bears. These animals were shown to the Roman crowds in zoos and circuses. During the Middle Ages, dancing bears became a familiar sight in European cities. Animal trainers were able to control a bear by fixing a ring through its nose, to which they fastened a long chain. They led the bear through the streets and trained it to walk on its hind legs much of the time. As the bear moved around to music, the trainers informed the crowds that it was "dancing."

The brown bear has been destroyed throughout much of Europe and Asia. Today a few of these animals live on in remote mountainous parts of Europe and in Russia.

Brown bears, just like Indians, Eskimos, and animals such as the elk, entered North America thousands of years ago. They traveled on a strip of land that connected Siberia in eastern Russia with Alaska. These bears changed in certain minor ways in their new home. Some acquired the silver-tipped fur that gives them the name grizzlies. The brown bears that live along the southern coast of Alaska and the Alaskan peninsula are now the largest land-dwelling carnivores in the world. A few of them weigh more than sixteen hundred pounds.

For most of the year the Alaskan brown bears live very much like their relatives, the grizzlies. They roam among the snow fields, rugged mountains, and fast-running streams on that beautiful coast and its islands. But in summer the streams are crowded with salmon. Then the Alaskan brown bears become fishermen.

No other kind of bear is so expert at fishing. They do not usually flip a fish out of the water with a front paw as most people think they do. Ben East, a writer who has often watched these bears, described how they do it.

"Their method is to pick a stretch of shallow water

where the stream runs over gravel or rocks, often at a rapids or low falls," East wrote. "There the bear stands watch until a salmon comes within reach. He pounces like a huge cat, sending water flying in every direction, pinning the fish on the bottom with a forepaw. Next he ducks his head under and grabs his prey in his jaws. He crunches or shakes the fish to break its spine. Then he carries it ashore and feeds, stripping off big slabs of flesh from both sides."

III

Asia has several species of black bears. One is called the Himalayan black bear, and it is a distant relative of the familiar black bear that lives in North America. This animal often makes its home in the high mountains of southern Asia, and has been found in summer at heights of eleven thousand feet. It is also a native of China and Japan.

The Himalayan black bear is not very large as bears go. An adult male may weigh a little over 250 pounds. But it is a fierce animal and has attacked human beings who disturbed it. Some writers believe that on its travels through the mountains it has helped to create legends about an Abominable Snowman.

This bear's appearance and habits are often curious.

It has a white chest patch, and the clump of long hair on its shoulders that protects it from wintry cold makes it seem as if it has a hump. In summer the bear often builds a nest of sticks in the trees, while in winter it builds its nest on the snow. It does not hibernate, as a rule. It seems to like to curl itself into a ball and roll down hills.

There are two other members of the black bear family that live in southern Asia. The sun bear inhabits the tropical forest, where it spends much time in trees. It is the smallest of the bears, seldom weighing more than 150 pounds. But it moves expertly up trees on its short, bowed legs, looking for small animals such as lizards and birds. If it finds a beehive, it sticks in its long tongue and licks up both honey and grubs. In good weather this bear sunbathes in a nest that it builds in the top of a tree.

The other black bear of southern Asia is called the sloth bear. Two hundred years ago, when hunters first sent its skin back to Europe, scientists didn't know what to make of this strange-looking animal from the jungles of India and Ceylon. They called it "the nameless animal." Some people thought it was a large sloth and not a bear. It has a dirty white muzzle and very long hair on the back of its neck and shoulders. A cub may ride on its mother's back, clinging to these long shoulder hairs. Its lips are thick and flabby.

The sloth bear climbs trees at night to rob birds' nests

or eat fruit. One of the sloth bear's favorite foods is termites. It breaks open a termite nest, sticks its head inside,
and twists its peculiar lips into a tube. Then it blows
furiously into the nest, clearing away the dust and trash,
and sucks up the termites. This makes a terrific racket,
and the sound of the bear's huffing and puffing, and snuf-
fling and slurping, can be heard a long distance away.

The spectacled bear is the only member of the family
that lives south of the equator. It roams the foothills of
the Andes in South America. This bear gets its name
from the big white or buff-colored patches around its eyes,
which make the animal look as if it is wearing spectacles.
A large male may weigh up to three hundred pounds, yet
it is an agile climber. It climbs some of the tallest trees
in the forest to find the leaves and fruits that form most
of its diet. The spectacled bear is now very rare because
human beings have cut down the forests where it makes
its home.

IV

Of all the bears, none is more widely admired than the
polar bear. The thick white fur that is tinged with light
yellow not only keeps the animal warm in its Arctic home,
but sets it apart from most of the other large animals in

the world. A person who could not tell a grizzly bear from a spectacled bear can immediately identify the big white bear of our northern lands.

The polar bear is well fitted for life in a land of snow. The dense coat keeps out the cold, while the short, stiff hairs on the bottoms of its feet keep the animal from slipping as it crosses its icy world. It is a powerful swimmer, paddling with only its front legs while its hind legs trail behind in the water. In rough seas it swims mostly under the waves, lifting its head now and then to breathe.

The polar bear is a splendid-looking animal as it comes from the sea, shaking itself vigorously like a dog so that the water does not cling to its fur and begin to freeze. Most bears have a solid, stubby body. This huge white bear, which may weigh up to one thousand pounds or more, has a sleek look. Its legs are longer than those of grizzlies and black bears. It has a long neck and a pointed muzzle, which looks in profile more like the curved beak of a bird of prey than the "dish" nose of the grizzly.

While the other members of the bear family are vegetarians much of the time, the polar bear is chiefly a meat eater. It feeds on animals that are as small as lemmings and young birds, or as large as seals. Swimming rapidly underwater, a polar bear sneaks up on a seal that is sleeping on the edge of the ice and kills it. A polar bear will also kill a small walrus, but avoids a large one because its tusks can inflict serious damage.

Cold weather does not frighten the polar bear. In periods when food is especially scarce, it may go into hibernation for a short time. But for most of the year, even in the dark of the Arctic winter, it wanders over the ice for great distances looking for food. If a dead whale is stranded on the ice, a dozen or more bears may come to feed on the carcass.

Scientists and their governments took strong action a few years ago to save the polar bear. For a long time this bear had seemed perfectly safe. Only the Eskimos hunted it, and they did not kill enough to endanger the population. There are no ranches or farms in the Arctic, so the polar bear was not considered a threat to anyone's domestic animals. The Arctic land was so remote from civilization that few hunters were able to reach there.

But modern inventions, mainly the airplane and snow-mobile, changed all that. Hunters found it easier to reach the Arctic. When they got there, they did not hunt the

---

The polar bear is chiefly a meat eater. It is a powerful hunter and feeds on animals as large as seals.

polar bear in a sportsmanlike manner, but used their machines to hunt them down.

In the Arctic regions of Alaska, Canada, and the Soviet Union, hunters began to kill hundreds of polar bears. One method was for the hunters to fly out over the ice in two small planes. When a bear was sighted, one of the planes landed and a hunter got out. He hid behind a hill of ice. The other plane flew low over the bear, frightening it and driving it toward the hidden hunter. The bear, confused and exhausted, had no chance against the hunter's high-powered rifle.

This form of sport disgusted many people. The bears were being killed simply because someone wanted a bear-skin rug to spread on the living-room floor. Scientists made their studies and found that the polar bear would eventually become extinct if this kind of hunting went on. Attempts to get hunters to change their methods failed.

Finally, the governments of all the countries that owned Arctic lands decided that the polar bear must be saved. The Soviet Union was the first to put an end to the hunting. The other nations followed. In 1972 the United States Congress passed the Marine Mammals Act, which was designed to protect whales, seals, and other animals that lived in and around the sea. The polar bear was given protection too. Hunting the bear was for-bidden. Even if an American hunter shot a polar bear in another country, he or she could not bring its skin into the United States.

Today it is very difficult for anyone, except certain Indians and Eskimos, to get permission to shoot a polar bear anywhere in the world. The only serious threat to its existence now comes from the oil drilling that is going on in Arctic waters. A big oil spill could kill many polar bears and other animals.

By working together, scientists and government officials have helped to preserve this endangered animal. It will not be as easy to save other kinds of bears. The spectacled bear is threatened because human beings are destroying the forests where it lives. The grizzly bear is threatened because some people believe it is too dangerous an animal. Even in the parks that have been set aside for wildlife, as we have seen, the grizzly bear is in trouble.

Can it survive in modern America?

9
BEARS IN OUR FUTURE

There are two pictures of bears that go on living in the minds of most people. There is the cuddly animal that served as a model for the teddy bear. There is also the bloodthirsty grizzly, rushing from the forest to strike down a camper. At first it seems that there is no way to use both of those images as we put together a true picture of bears.

Yet such opposite views tell us a great deal about these animals. There are so many ways in which a bear may behave that we cannot be certain what it is really like. Much depends on the size of the animal, where it lives, and how human beings have acted toward it. A bear is one of the most interesting animals because it shows us so many different faces.

The wild bear is not the bumbling "Yogi Bear" of the

cartoons. Nor is it the dreadful monster of the horror movies. It isn't even the lazy, contented animal that looks bored behind bars at the zoo. The wild bear lives in a harsh environment where it must work hard to survive.

When that environment changes, this intelligent animal changes too. If the summer's berry crop is poor, the bear digs roots or eats grass. If tourists provide handouts, or if ranchers fill their fields with helpless young calves, the bear eagerly turns to this easy way of making a living. In either of these cases, the bear naturally will take more than the human beings want to let it have. Then the trouble begins.

Grizzlies, as we have seen, are large enough and strong enough to keep on taking what they want. These bears often lose their fear of humans, but not their fierceness. When that happens, we hear about campers being attacked or livestock being destroyed.

Today the grizzly cannot live in most parts of the United States. California and its other old feeding grounds have become too crowded with people. Sooner or later a human disturbs a grizzly and is killed or injured. Our civilization will tolerate thousands of people being killed by cars, planes, and motorcycles. But it will not tolerate even a few people being killed by wild animals. The bears, as a result, are driven away from places where people live in large numbers.

A black bear, drugged by scientists, lies under a blanket on the snow. The scientists will make a record of the animal's temperature and physical condition.

There is only one region wild and rugged enough for grizzlies in the lower forty-eight states. That is the high country in Montana, Wyoming, and Idaho. There, if we care enough to keep this living symbol of the Old West, the grizzly bear can still find a home.

Scientists and government officials are working hard to keep the grizzly there. An Interagency Study Team has been formed, composed of scientists from state and federal agencies. They are looking for ways to prevent clashes between people and the grizzly.

This will not be easy. Some areas of our national parks and forests may have to be closed to campers and hikers. Ranchers may have to keep their cattle off the grazing lands in parts of the national forests. The grizzly needs some place of its own where it can live as it did before civilization caught up with it. If we cannot make room for the grizzly, it will disappear from this region too. Then, in the future, grizzlies will be found only in a few wild places in Canada and Alaska.

The black bears and human beings have learned to live a little better with each other. Still, most states with black bears need tighter restrictions on hunting them.

Bears need lots of room. Giving them a place to live is the key to keeping bears in our future.

Bears do not reproduce every year, and so they will not recover from excessive hunting as quickly as many other mammals do.

This black bear is the animal that the reader may see on visits to large parks in many parts of the country. Even if the black bear is not seen, there will be signs of its presence. Rangers will offer advice to all campers and tourists about how to behave with bears. If people use common sense and keep their distance from these animals, there is not likely to be trouble.

There is an old story about a man who followed bear tracks in the snow. After a while he gave up. When a friend asked him why he had not gone on, he replied:

"Those tracks were getting too darn fresh!"

That is a good point to keep in mind in our dealings with bears. We can follow their lives with curiosity and respect. But providing them with a space of their own is the key to keeping bears in our future.

ACKNOWLEDGMENTS

The following books were extremely useful to us in our research:

Craighead, Frank C., Jr. *Track of the Grizzly*. San Francisco: Sierra Club Books, 1979.

East, Ben. *Bears*. New York: Crown Publishers, 1977.

Leopold, Aldo. *A Sand County Almanac*. New York: Oxford University Press, 1949.

Murie, Adolph. *A Naturalist in Alaska*. Old Greenwich, Conn.: Devin-Adair Company, 1961.

Murie, Olaus J. *A Field Guide to Animal Tracks*. Boston: Houghton Mifflin Company, 1954.

Schullery, Paul. *The Bears of Yellowstone*. Yellowstone National Park: Yellowstone Library and Museum Association, 1980.

Acknowledgments

Storer, Tracy I., and Tevis, Lloyd P., Jr. *California Grizzly*. Lincoln, Neb.: University of Nebraska Press, 1978.

We would especially like to thank Paul Schullery for his many courtesies while we were writing this book.
—ADA AND FRANK GRAHAM

INDEX

Index

Frank Graham is a field editor of *Audubon* and one of the nation's leading naturalists. He is the author of a number of books about conservation including *Since Silent Spring* and *Disaster by Default: Politics and Water Pollution.*

Ada Graham is a teacher-naturalist and the author with her husband of the five previous Audubon Readers, each of which was named an Outstanding Science Trade Book for Children by the National Science Teachers Association. *Whale Watch*, Audubon Reader #1, was an ALA Notable Children's Book. The Grahams live in Milbridge, Maine.

D. D. Tyler, who has illustrated the other Audubon Readers, is a painter and illustrator of wildlife subjects. She has been a staff artist for the *Maine Times* and lives with her husband, a naturalist, and her son in Augusta, Maine.